Conservatism

A New Modest Proposal

By Max Humana

Reality Publishing, LLC

Conservastan (A New Modest Proposal) 1st Edition.

Published by Reality Publishing, LLC.
Copyright © 2019, Reality Publishing, LLC.

For more information, contact Reality Publishing, LLC at realitypublishing2100@gmail.com.

Cover design by Max Humana.

ISBN: 978-1-7332857-3-5

Other Books By The Author

Thank god For Eve; Why Religion Exists And Why It Must Go

America As A Case Study In The Harmful Effects of Religion (Chapter Six from the book *Thank god For Eve* as a separate pamphlet)

An Opening Salvo On Coexistence; Plus Everybody's An Atheist And I Can Prove It (Chapter Eleven from the book *Thank god For Eve* as a separate pamphlet)

Thou Shalt Not Think; How Psychology Subverts Reason And Opens Pandora's Box of Faith (Chapter Twelve from the book *Thank god For Eve* as a separate pamphlet)

Religions Are Fruitful, They Multiply, And They Are Very Bad For You (Chapter Fifteen from the book *Thank god For Eve* as a separate pamphlet)

Why Is Any Moral Person Still A Catholic? (The Church of Evil, Abnormality and Hypocrisy) (Chapter Twenty-One from the book *Thank god For Eve* as a separate pamphlet)

America's Completely Secular Founding Documents (More Christian Attempts At Rewriting History) (Chapter Twenty-Seven from the book *Thank god For Eve* as a separate pamphlet)

Religious Freedom Laws, Also Known As "My god Says You're A Piece of Shit" (Chapter Twenty-Eight from the book *Thank god For Eve* as a separate pamphlet)

Four Degrees of Separation

Trump Voters: Ignorance, Stupidity and Evil

Dedication

Fascism, racism, bigotry, xenophobia, intolerance, mindless tribalism, genocide and other such antihuman behaviors are not new. The words are new, but the actions and attitudes have been a part of our species for millennia. Untold numbers of people have been demonized, persecuted, imprisoned, beaten, tortured, exiled and killed throughout human history by those with much in the way of ignorance, stupidity, evil and sadism but very little intelligence, wisdom or morality.

These people have been responsible for hate crimes, slavery, pogroms, heresy hunts, purges, Crusades, Inquisitions, individual murders, large scale mass murders and the destruction of everything from independent thought to the science of their time to living human beings.

These people are still among us, as recent events such as the American slave trade, the Holocaust and the American presidential election in 2016 have demonstrated. There are far too many such people even in places like the modern USA. As long as these people are allowed to spread their ignorance, stupidity and evil, innocent people will suffer and die. Those of us who are intelligent, compassionate and moral are beyond tired of living with these ignorant and immoral sadists.

This book is dedicated to all the brave, moral and decent people who fight against such ignorance and evil wherever and whenever it is encountered. The rise of fascism and authoritarian dictators can only be stopped by those of honorable mental and moral character who take action to preserve humanity and a civil society. I dedicate this book to all such patriots everywhere.

Contents

Contents

Conservastan
A New Modest Proposal

"Mark my word, if and when these preachers get control of the [Republican] party, and they're sure trying to do so, it's going to be a terrible damn problem. Frankly, these people frighten me. Politics and governing demand compromise. But these Christians believe they are acting in the name of God, so they can't and won't compromise. I know, I've tried to deal with them."

- Barry Goldwater, American Republican politician from the 1950s through the 1980s

Were you ever in a doomed relationship? Most of us have been in that situation at least once, even if it's one that never included a domestic disturbance call to the police. Maybe it was one of those nonexplosive situations where the two parties still mostly get along, but their lives slowly and inexorably diverged. In those cases the dynamic usually becomes too much to ignore, and at least one of the partners finds a way to end the relationship.

These breakups often occur with a whimper and not a bang, which in a nation like the US, with its insatiable fetish for guns, is an extremely good thing.

There can also be situations in which one partner does or says something terribly damaging or evil that permanently and immediately torpedoes the relationship. Physical or sexual abuse of a family member, infidelity, major deceit, commission of a violent crime or any of a number of other undesirable behaviors are often first-time-offense unforgivable and will quickly end a relationship. In these cases, things can indeed end with an actual bang, from an actual gun.

And then there are cases where one of the partners simply goes off his or her rocker and starts saying and/or doing things that make no sense, and might not be immediate deal-breakers but will be fatal to the relationship if continued. Perhaps a partner develops a gambling, drinking or drug habit. Or they decide they want to spend all the couple's money on fripperies. Or they join a religious cult that believes in giving away all the couple's possessions and moving to a mountaintop, or they start insisting that only prayer can heal sick children.

Such stupidities, if continued against the other partner's strongly expressed wishes, are relationship-enders, and healthy and sane persons don't allow them in their relationships.

The situation in the United States following the presidential election in November 2016 is either at or has already passed the point of no return when it comes to governance, civility and indeed coexistence, at least in the legislative sphere. Try to find a more dysfunctional group than the US Congress. A more ineffective and feckless display of entrenched and blind hyperpartisanship would be hard to find outside of a fundamentalist / evangelical church or a sports stadium filled with drunken partisans.

But those well-remunerated people on the Hill aren't being paid to warm seats and root for the home team to win a meaningless game or to score points with their imaginary god of choice. They are public servants, meaning they are our employees, and they are being paid very handsome sums of taxpayer money to conduct the nation's business and to work for the best interests of *all* of its citizens. Not just some of them, not just those who voted for them, but all of them. Even the ones who voted for the other party and would never cross a partisan line.

And let there be no weak-kneed Neville Chamberlainish talk of equivalence here, as this is absolutely not a 'both sides do it just as much' issue. Republicans in Congress have failed to uphold their office and their oath. They have devolved to operating in feral packs of special interest groups funded by uberpartisans and theocratic power-hungry rapacious oligarchs and enemies *both foreign and domestic* who absolutely do not have the best interests of everyone in mind, and they deliberately work to serve only the very narrow goals of a few check-writers, influence peddlers and selfish ideologues.

Republican politicians in America today are astoundingly immoral and unethical and are determined to perpetrate their immoral and antihuman schemes on the American people, with their primary targets being the most vulnerable among us.

Ever since Bill Clinton was elected, Republicans have been screaming "The world is ending! The world is ending!" without any actual factual basis for any of their insane blathering. Much of his presidency was subject to the constant background din of a flock of frantically screaming red-state Chicken Littles, whining

3

and crying "woe is me!" and "woe is us!" and "we have to impeach!"

Then Clinton left office and we were subjected to an unbelievably incompetent eight years of a so-called president and presidency determined to stake its claim as one of the very worst in the history of the country. For eight years, Republicans had things pretty much their own way, "led" by a shiftless former drunk and theocrat who couldn't even speak or spell the word 'presidential', much less actually do the job.

That experiment in unhinged, dogmatic and fact-free conservative politico-theology run riot resulted in two lost wars, trillions of dollars of wasted money, decades of national budgets blown to utter hell, thousands upon thousands of the bodies, brains and psyches of American men and women in uniform similarly blown to hell, continuous fearmongering, numerous Constitutional problems, textbook cases of how to utterly fail to properly respond to natural disasters, and a financial and economic crisis of truly apocalyptic proportions. That lost decade set the country back in practically every positive measurable known to man.

And Republicans from the poorhouse to the penthouse, from the state to the federal level, demonstrating their abilities to lie reflexively and completely deny reality, *still* say it wasn't that bad.

Thoughtful Americans responded in the next election by choosing the absolute polar opposite of Duhbya Bush – an extremely intelligent, highly educated, thoughtful, empathic, perceptive, studious, forward-thinking, hard-working and inclusive leader who had the best interests of all of America and indeed of all Americans in mind from Day One. He also happened to be partly black.

Since almost no Republicans in the last few decades who were either elected to office or who have been part of any local or national discourse possess even a single one of the positive characteristics listed above, the pachyderm party faithful's already well-entrenched penis envy, xenophobic faith-based bigotry and mindless insecurities blasted into stratospheric overdrive.

For the new President to be not just Democratic, but for him to have the audacity to be even half black ("He's black, Ethel, *black*! Can you believe it?!") was just too much, adding insult to the already gravely injured collective red-state psyche. In the true spirit of hate and intolerance that is personified in American conservatives today in so many ugly ways, these developments caused them to retreat into a tight ball of full fetal position infantilism.

They individually, collectively and quite openly stated they would do nothing for the new President's entire tenure except to childishly whine "No!", fold their arms and hold their breath, then block and obstruct every positive action that was proposed, even if it had been originally and recently dreamed up or proposed by a Republican and still had the damn "Made by GOP" sticker on it.

Adding grave insult to Constitutional, ethical and moral injury, Mitch McConnell has used his time as Senate Majority Leader to make it publicly and privately known that he has been and will continue to block progress and stifle legislative improvements, and he has done this very vigorously. In 2019 this individual actually and unbelievably stopped progress on election security measures, despite such action being of grave importance to national integrity and national security.

All of these numerous anti-American acts of omission and commission, some of which are actually acts of de facto collusion with Russia, one of our most dedicated global adversaries, have earned him the highly-deserved nickname "Moscow Mitch". And this is the Senate Majority Leader. The rot is well and truly all the way through to the core in the GOP.

During Barack Obama's presidency, Republicans in Congress did everything in their power[1] to fight, block, subvert, destroy[2] and reverse every bit of pro-human and pro-environment progress he accomplished or sought to accomplish. Again, this even included ideas *originally proposed by Republicans*. This is not quite treasonous but it is a deliberate violation of the sacred oath these Republicans faithlessly and disingenuously swore when they took office. That oath requires them to support and defend the Constitution **and** the people of this country. What a sorry, pitiful lot. They deserve both full-throated contempt and immediate removal from office.

The rhetoric of the red-staters and the pathetic gaggle of laughable and patently unqualified incompetents they paraded as so-called 'candidates' during the 2016 presidential campaign made it clear that they fully intended to continue in obstructionism at all costs if the election went blue again.

Republicans of the last several decades have not been principled representatives of a 'conservative perspective' on governance, seeking solutions which benefit both the common man and woman and the business community.

They have not been open to reasonable compromise and responsible governance. They began selling their souls long ago, and are now in complete and utter thrall to the twin devils of money and power.

They spend like drunken sailors on needless wars and tax cuts for wealthy corporations and the extremely rich, but scream about the deficit and the dire and immediate need for fiscal restraint while they do their evil damnedest to cut funding for programs which enable women, children, the elderly and the sick to eat and to have affordable medical care.

And now they aren't even trying to hide the obstructionism, the abdication of the duties to which they were elected and which are contained within that solemn oath which they knew they would violate even as they mouthed the words. The right-wing obstructionists in Congress and the right-wing media are in complete collusion in this, and they are now actively fostering a self-perpetuating feedback loop in which the Congress, conservative media and the general population in red states are becoming ever more brazen and bold in their own particular obstructionism.

This has led to ranchers occupying federal facilities, armed self-professed militia members entering American cities and pretending to be a 'stabilizing influence', disgraced so-called "judges" in Alabama and county clerks in the reddest and most ignorant parts of America telling the Supreme Court and the Constitution they rode in on to screw off in the name of their particular pet god. All with the full support of many of the 2016 Republican presidential candidates and sitting GOP congresscreatures.

But how do such pig-headed, uncompromising and actually evil specimens get into office? They are voted in by ignorant, stupid and evil people who have drunk the Kool-Aid, believed the lies, and are themselves too ignorant, stupid and/or evil to realize that they have swallowed both the short and long cons, hook, line and toxic lead sinker. And with the state of mind and education in the country falling as far as it has, it is unlikely that this problem will reverse itself without a major existential and external threat far worse than some piddling Islamic terrorist threat.

The American right wing itself is currently a major terroristic and national security threat to the population of the United States, having killed or injured far more Americans through deregulation, unnecessary wars, domestic terrorism, benefit cuts, pollution, hate-crime murders and other actions than any Islamic or other non-right-wing terrorists have killed.

Simply put, we now have incontrovertible proof that we can count on conservative Americans to vote for the exact wrong people to fill seats in our halls of elected power. Look around the country for a sickening display of the inability of these voters to cast a responsible ballot. Trump, Pence, Cruz, Rubio, Inhofe, McConnell, Gingrich, Hastert, McCarthy, Boehner, Hensarling, Abbott, Perry, Palin, Bush, Nunes, Ryan, Cheney, Huckabee, Gohmert, Mulvaney, the Tea Party, the horrifically misnamed "Freedom" Caucus, Roy Moore, Orrin Hatch, Santorum, Jindal, Brownback, Christie, the list just goes on and on and on, like a Satanic Who's Who of intolerance, ignorance and evil.

As the ignorant, stupid and evil population who elected these liars, fools and fascists has children and indoctrinates them to be the new generation of ignorant, stupid and evil voters, it is highly likely that the cementation of hyperpartisanship and the bankrupt policies of the GOP, despite galactic levels of factual evidence of their failure, will continue unchecked.

The real question is, do these politicians actually believe what they say and have permanently and totally firewalled themselves off from evidence proving they are wrong? Or do they know they are completely wrong and just spout the talking points to feed the population daily doses of drugged red meat in their pursuit of personal power and riches and doing sadistic and unchristian evil to the poor? No matter how many people are hurt in the end? It is surely often both, sometimes in the same person. And it is safe to assume the worst, because the words and deeds of these hateful people are certainly intended for the worst outcomes for people.

Their media are equally dead to reality and are beholden to fascism and intolerance, not to mention the craziest of crazy conspiracy theories. Hugh Hewitt, Mark Levin, Rush Limbaugh, Alex Jones, Breitbart, almost everyone in front of and behind the cameras at the tragically misnamed far right-wing and often fact-free Fox "News", Coulter, Blaze, and indeed the entire frothing and angry constellation of right-wingers on conservative media, are all doing whatever they can to balkanize, to demonize and then to monetize our differences, this last being their true goal.

This list too could go on for many painful days, but the point is made. Goldwater's fears of the xenophobic and sadistic Old Testament-motivated faithful have come true. The religious right has thoroughly contaminated Republican politics. Both the pulpits and the halls of power echo with their hatred and evil. None of these people seek compromise. They seek to have things 100% their own way, and are almost universally devoid of even a shred of proven and verified empirical evidence for their positions.

If you are on the other side, you are denigrated personally and professionally, and are designated as a target for vitriol and attacks from virtual to verbal to physical, and death threats are common. That this is a modern day repetition of the slow decline to the thuggish fascism and Holocaustic outcomes of 20th century Europe is completely lost on these people.

Or is it? We may soon find out, and November 2020 will be a Rubicon for this country.

And just as masses of Germans and Italians were led by hateful demagogues to national fascism and acts of supreme evil, today's American conservatives are extremely easily led down the path to bigotry, hatred and even violence by hateful and divisive rhetoric, although this is denied loudly and without any hint of acceptance of responsibility. Conservatives in America today are psychologically primed for hatred and violence, with a bloody trail of death threats, abortion clinic[3] and innocent bystander[4] shootings as proof.

The actual murders, death threats and massive spikes in intimidations and other violence which resulted from the unbelievable bigotry of Trump and Pence and their hateful and Nazi-like rhetoric both before and after the election are now extremely well-documented. Right-wing bigotry, and indeed right-wing domestic terrorism, is alive and well after being reinvigorated by Trump's vicious rhetoric, and it is flourishing in the nation's media, the general population and the Congress like a malicious and deadly virus.

Texas has long blathered about its being 'a whole other country'. If you have ever spent any time there, you will of course find plenty of decent, honest, good and law-abiding citizens who respect the letter and the spirit of the law, the Constitutional separation of church and state, and will actually vote for candidates who didn't just step off the pages of the Old Testament, bloody sword in hand. But in much of Texas, and indeed in vast swaths of the South, where from 2008-2016 the sentiment was "Obahma ain't *mah* predisent!", there are massive amounts of people both in and out of government down there who do indeed think and act like they are their own country.

To them, the Constitution is just a bunch of highfalutin' words written by some dead Yanks, and 'nuttin' to trouble theyselves with if it don't agree none with'n how they want things done', except of course their incessant repetition of the Most Holy Second 'Amemmunt'. And their rhetoric can reach the fever pitch of a true believer, complete with clenched fists, raised Bibles, sweaty brows and calls for some kind of righteous cleansing, be it ethnic or some other kind.

The rhetoric, and indeed the entire national relationship, has reached the point where we as a nation need to start thinking about bypassing the trial separation stage and going to a full and permanent divorce. Unless there is a major change by the right-wing fascists, demagogues and intolerants who are holding the country hostage, which at the moment seems quite impossible, this marriage will not be saved.

The true test of this fracturing national concord will be the 2020 elections. If things don't get far more reasonable during that potential watershed event, it will be time to separate the assets and have the parties go in their own directions, hopefully with more emphasis on "civil" than "war" in the process.

So what are the differences between the two sides? There are many, but they center on an inability to agree on issues of immense importance not just to individual Americans, but to the population of the entire country, and indeed all humans on earth and the very biosphere we inhabit. What are these issues, and why are they important? A sampling is listed below, in no particular order, along with the differences between the antihuman unjustified Republican opinions and the differing conclusions held by those who base their positions on facts, reality, the Constitution and actual humanistic morality.

1. **Economy and Taxes.**
    - Republicans either actually do or pretend to strongly believe in the permanently and completely false and continually-debunked nonsensical dogmas of "trickle down" voodoo economics, regressive taxation and tax "policy" designed specifically to favor the rich, wealthy campaign contributors and large wealthy corporations, along with policies which have been repeatedly and tragically proven to massively increase income inequality and destroy budgets and economies. The history of their disastrous and antihuman tax code changes continues to illuminate their true motivations in precise detail. These disastrous Republican tax and economic policies have always resulted in reduced well-being for the vast majority of people while a very few become wealthy, along with astronomically expanded state and national deficits which they scream are terrible

12

until they get into office and make them worse. The utter hypocrisy of a party stating it is for a small government and fiscal restraint while massively expanding the size and power of the government while borrowing from China to spend like a fleet of drunken sailors is obvious to everyone. Today's Republicans are a combination of utter incompetents and pathological liars.

- Progressives and independents favor a responsible system of appropriate economic management, blending capitalist drive with appropriately providing for the good of all citizens, plus a goal of lessening income inequality, ensuring an economically and historically-proven tax code is implemented and having a safety net for those who truly need it.

2. **Minimum / Living Wage.**
   - Republicans say an increase in the minimum wage would destroy the American economy, yet income inequality is at historic levels and only a few individuals have half of the nation's wealth. Far too many people labor at multiple low-paying jobs and often without benefits while corporations and their executives take billions of dollars in government subsidies and other programs while making their workers use federally-funded programs to make ends meet. In other words, rapacious corporations rake in profits, don't pay them to their workers and make taxpayers fund the wages and/or benefits the companies could provide but choose not to.

   - Progressives and independents know there is easily enough wealth to enable workers to receive a living wage and for the national economic system to enable a decent living without having to work multiple jobs. With a tiny handful of billionaires now owning most of the world's wealth and increasing numbers of people living paycheck to paycheck or not even that well, there is no excuse for plutocratic rule except

Republican sadism and their thoroughly anti-Christian sadistic greed.

3. **Wall Street.**
    *   Republicans worship their god and their guns and their money, and those in Congress and rapacious businesses are in absolute knees-in-dirt worshipful thrall to the greedy gluttons on Wall Street who say they don't ever need regulation despite recent and massively catastrophic evidence that they can't be trusted to even be legal, much less moral. They also think that regular people – meaning those who are not wealthy - who disagree with them can just screw off and die.

    *   Progressives and independents, with extremely notable exceptions such as Hillary Clinton and others who have found fortune with Wall Street and wish to keep the money flowing, know and have proven that in general Wall Street is a bunch of greedy capitalists who break or bend laws and words wherever and whenever they can to enrich themselves and who demonstrate on a daily basis just how badly they do need massive amounts of strict oversight and regulation.

4. **International Terrorism.**
    *   The terrified snowflakes on the right quiver in continuous fear that countless cabals of international terrorists all around the world are constantly planning to invade and destroy America, and these frightened fools spend not billions but trillions of dollars on endless wars, an elephantine and not very effective homeland security apparatus and screwing with other people's governments while sneering at diplomacy that doesn't come from the barrel of a gun.

    *   Progressives and independents generally understand the true causes of terrorism and work to address them while taking the minimum level of military action

14

that needs to be promulgated, although some are blinded by being overly and uncritically empathetic and "multicultural" toward people who are factually and incorrigibly evil.

5. **War.**

- Republicans love conflict, they have strong sadistic streaks and they get twitchy if the country goes more than a few weeks without a war. All one need do to prove this is to listen to what they say and observe what they do. The USA is one of the most warlike countries on earth, from economic wars to trade wars to actual shooting wars. The words "war" and "battle" and "fight" are ubiquitous in the right wing's lexicon. Republicans absolutely love wars, and are happy to keep them going as long as *other people* and *other people's kids* are on the front lines and not themselves or their own kids. Republicans in elected office, as the cowards and hypocritical sadists they are, always find ways to send the nation's poor to war without sending any of their own kids or going themselves. Republican administrations and Congress are clear and continuously proven evidence of this.

- Progressives and independents prefer to use force as a last resort due to the immense human, social and financial costs. They know that the instruments of national power include economic, diplomatic and other means rather than a shooting war. They also know that it is immoral and antihuman to go to war with or have alliances with other nations simply to have temporary access to finite natural resources such as oil. They also know the many long-term consequences of wars, unlike Republicans who can't be bothered to think about anything beyond catchphrases such as "the Iraqis will pay us back for the war" or "we're fighting for freedom" or "Mission Accomplished" when the facts show all of their conservo-religious promises to be lies.

6. **International Relations.** Also see "International Terrorism" and "War" above.
   - Republicans are also blind to or they deliberately ignore the fact that the continuous stream of political and military interventions which the US has started or participated in over just the last 50 years has itself been a driving force for the growth of anti-Americanism and terrorism. Progressives and independents clearly see this problem and they seek to address global security challenges and national objectives through a judicious application of the appropriate elements of national power.

   - Republicans think the way to convert the rest of the world to their hyperconstricted and uninformed ways of thinking is through the barrel of a gun, which is exactly what one of the most evil humans in history, Mao Zedong, said ("Political power grows out of the barrel of a gun"). Progressives and independents know there is a time to use guns, and it is best exemplified in the expression "speak softly and carry a big stick", which when wielded should be put to maximum effect and efficiency. One need not beat so many places so often with that stick as Republicans love to do, as they, again, never put their own cowardly skins on the line and as they use other people's children to do it.

7. **Domestic Terrorism.**
   - The Republican right wing in America today is essentially sole-sourcing domestic terrorism[5] on a continuous basis. It denies this and denies its existence despite actively and deliberately fomenting its rise, along with the simultaneous and mutually supporting rise of white nationalism. In other words, right-wing American citizens are waging a low-level war on other Americans simply due to the color of their skin, their political affiliation, their religion or lack thereof, or some wholly imaginary full-on bat-shit crazy lunatic fringe Alex Jones or Breitbart-level

belief like Hillary Clinton running a sex ring out of a pizza shop. If you think that sort of thing is too stupid-crazy that anyone could actually believe it, you need to spend some time reading, watching and listening to right-wing media.

There literally is no limit to the unbelievably incoherent insanity that masses of Republicans in and out of office will either actually believe or will spread to the ignorant, fearful and compliant conservative masses. These unthinking drones gulp down the toxic Kool-Aid from their leaders and propagandists without question, like baby birds happily receiving partly-digested vomit down their yawning gapes.

- Progressives and independents rightly see this threat[6] and work to lessen and mitigate it but are often threatened by or actually become victims of the threat, often just because they pointed it out. With Republicans often in charge of one or more branches of the government, and with their own rhetoric often contributing to the problem, those working against the causes and spread of domestic terrorism and its spirit partner white nationalism are being deliberately blocked, as described above in the section on GOP intransigence.

8. **Separation Of Church And State.**
- Republicans, particularly after the party's full and complete takeover by fascistic and insane theocratic ideologies and eschatologies starting in the 1980s and at least to this point culminating with their coronation of their god-king-president in 2017, have done **exactly** what Barry Goldwater feared. The quote from him in the epigraph at the start of this book clearly shows that this strong conservative, who if he were alive today would be denigrated and ridiculed by the entire GOP as Republican In Name Only (RINO) and a squishy pathetic liberal, was far more intelligent and perceptive and far less psychopathic

than the masses of Republicans in the pews, pulpits and elective offices today. Republicans deliberately and continually work to violate the Constitution they pray to so loudly and unbiblically in public, against Jesus's direct guidance not to do so (Matthew 6:5 through 6:7; KJV), by breaking down the Constitutional separation between church and state and seeking to turn the American government into a Christian theocracy at all levels. The GOP is a clear and present danger to the population. It is a direct threat to the sanctity of the secular foundation of our country and the Constitutional separation of church and state which was very specifically and very intentionally woven into the nation's founding ethos and its founding documents.

- Progressives and independents want to maintain the strong and permanent separation from church and state and a permanent and unbroken continuation of our strongly secular Constitution. This is not merely because to do so is Constitutional and by doing so it is following the law, but because mountains of empirical evidence show that secular nations[7] are demonstrably happier, safer, more altruistic and generally better off in numerous objective and subjective ways. And progressives are keenly aware of the oceans of innocent blood which the religious and conservatives throughout history, both at home and abroad, have spilled and will assuredly continue to spill whenever they are in charge, and they wish to avoid this.

9. **Women's Rights**.
   - Republicans and conservatives feel this expression is an oxymoron, and are opposed to so-called "uppity", feminist or even independent women in general. In other words, they feel women should be restrained to the "rights" to bear children, to maintain the household and do man's bidding, just like it says in their bible. Conservatives were the ones who fought

tooth and nail against women's rights and sought to keep them barefoot, pregnant and quiet. Conservatives, especially the most religious ones, insisted women were not smart or competent enough to vote. As a result, women achieved suffrage only after a protracted fight against entrenched, occasionally violent and always thoroughly immoral religious and conservative opposition.

- Independents and progressives support the full equality of women and men, to include fair and equal pay, employment and educational opportunities, and to be free of harassment and unfair discrimination of any kind. They reject the use of ancient fairy tales of sadism, discrimination and misogyny to justify modern sadism, discrimination and misogyny. They embrace Enlightenment values, not Inquisitional values.

10. Birth Control / Family Planning.

- While opinions vary greatly, a fair generalization would be that the Republican right, due to its extreme religiosity and perception of women as second-class citizens, believes all these practices are wrong or 'sinful', and would criminalize them if it could. Just as it has been doing for generations in America, it is waging an extremely aggressive and underhanded anti-reproductive rights campaign across the country, and it will continue to do so until its particular religious strain of anti-female immorality is unconstitutionally embedded in our legal code.

- Progressives and independents, for practical, humanistic and moral reasons, know that being responsible in birth control and family planning practices are truly moral, proper and pro-social actions, and support them in all times and all places. They also know that educating young people on how their bodies work and not shaming them for having genitalia or the desire to use them is the truly moral and rational path. They know that ignorance, particularly faith-based ignorance and denials of science and reality, solves no problems.

11. **Child Abuse, Children's Rights and Parenting.**
- Republicans often treat children in true 'spare the rod and spoil the child' biblical fashion, subject to whatever 'punishment' or 'parenting' style their parents and elders deem appropriate. Indeed, their disgustingly anti-child ethos is in plain language, in stark black and white[8] and *in their own evil words*. The 2012 Texas Republican Party Platform Committee Report states, unbelievably and ironically in the "PROTECTING OUR CHILDREN" section, that "We unequivocally oppose the United States Senate's ratification of the United Nations Convention on the Rights of the Child." Yes, unbelievably, Republicans *unequivocally oppose* the following words from the Convention intended to protect children:

  > "...childhood is entitled to special care and assistance..."

  > Children "...should grow up in a family environment, in an atmosphere of happiness, love and understanding..."

  > Children should be raised in a society "...in the spirit of peace, dignity, tolerance, freedom, equality and solidarity..."

- Progressives, independents and factually anyone with a working brain and a molecule of either common sense or morality are speechless at the sadistic and immoral hatred and tyranny which conservatives wield to remove the Freedom of a child to grow up in a loving, nurturing and fear-free environment. It is utterly unconscionable to raise children in the totalitarian and sadistic ethos which Christian

20

Republicans espouse. This is why so many of their children are raised in emotionally and physically abusive situations.

12. **Education / Charter Schools.**

- The key to a truly healthy, happy and prosperous modern civilization is a very high-quality education for its citizenry. This education must be broad, cover many subjects and absolutely must be based on facts, reality, truth, observation and critical thinking. Far from independent thinking or a proper multiperspective and holistic education, Republicans want only their side and their perspective inculcated, regardless of the lies and dogmas they contain. They reject or twist facts as needed so they can fit into their skewed version of a preferred alternate reality in which Big Brother has killed off reason and truth and only Republican lies and dogma are allowed. This is not mere opinion; they again astoundingly state this position quite clearly and in public.

  To Republicans, critical or independent thinking is abhorrent[9] and they strongly oppose it, both verbally and in print. They continue to profess, even after countless disastrous failures and wholly falsified snake oil promises,[10] that if they just keep trying the failed charter school approach that someday it will perform as advertised. Insanity is doing something again and again while hoping for a different result. Republicans are clearly insane on this subject, and/or they aren't but are doing a damn good job of faking it, and/or they are yet again playing the rubes to enrich themselves and pander to a religiously stupefied electorate. Undoubtedly all are true to some extent.

- Progressives and independents know the facts. They know that a good education is essential to properly understanding and living in the world and to maximizing one's potential. They know that for many children an education may be the only means they have to achieve their dreams, be it the "American Dream" or any other. While Republicans work hard from the state and local to the national levels to dilute and water down education and make getting an education harder, progressives fight to increase the quality and access to education for all citizens. Without this education, the primary key to maximal human freedom and independence is largely lost. That last is in fact the Republican goal; they are working hard to turn most Americans into uneducated and ignorant drones who unhesitatingly, and ignorantly, follow their dear leaders' every command.

13. **Abortion.**
   - In general, conservatives don't feel that anything between a newly-fertilized egg or a seconds-from-delivery baby should be considered for abortion. Many of them strongly believe this even when the pregnancy is potentially fatal to the mother, if the child has a terminal health problem and is going to die anyway or if the pregnant female is a nine year old girl who had been raped by her stepfather.[11] Many Republicans actually and astoundingly hold the idiotic belief that most women use abortions as a method of birth control. This unhinged and woman-insulting sadistic blinding to reality and true human morality by religion is a constant theme with Republicans. Also, since between 50 and 70 percent of human embryos naturally abort, these religious Republicans need to start understanding biological science and asking their god why it lets so many natural abortions happen.

   - Progressives have differing perspectives on abortion, and the vast majority strongly feel it is always a thing to be avoided if possible. But they almost universally support very early to early stage abortions, and for a great many of them the support for abortion continues to decrease the nearer the fetus approaches viability. They support exceptions for rape, incest, health of the mother or if the fetus is going to die due to some terminal defect or malformation. If a female has been raped or her life is in danger, she alone should have the decision as to what to do with her pregnancy, at least until the latest stages.

And it is extremely important to note the unbelievably arrogant and again sadistic hypocrisy which Republicans display with regard to babies immediately *after* they are born. Their frenzied over-the-top defense of the unborn ceases at the microsecond the newborn's umbilical is cut, at which time they see the new child as just another 'taker', an unwelcome probable welfare recipient who will need to be denied social services, health care, education and a living wage.

14. **Science.**

- Republicans generally do not believe in or trust science, as it always disproves their pet religious, political and social beliefs and dogmas, and frankly because most of them don't have the intellectual capacity to understand it. Progressives don't use the word "believe" when referring to science; they know that science actually works, that it provides the only source of actual knowledge we have, and that evidence and truth are actually real, even if disturbing or disagreeable. Progressives use and rely on science because it is the only system of human activity that has been proven to discover the actual truth about our world.

- To a conservative, an 'alternative fact' is escapism and a safe room they think they can run into when they want to hide from the truths of science. It is an attempted way out of facing an inconvenient or uncomfortable scientific truth or an objective reality. To a progressive and any honest person who values the truth, the so-called 'alternative fact' is a false statement, that is to say it is a lie, stated either through ignorance or the far more prevalent use as a deliberate intent to deceive.

- Conservatives reap the benefits of science when it suits them, but ignore or deny science when it does not, as when murderous jihadis use technology to fly airplanes into buildings while denying evolution, and when American Christians try to inject creationism and religion into the school system and our laws while denying essentially the whole of biological and physical science. Conservatives scream endlessly about the so-called immorality of homosexuality, while rejoicing and praising their god and elected officials when kids are thrown into cages, and while protecting child rapists such as the priests of the Catholic cult. Such science denial and dogma is the antithesis of the scientific model and exposes the omnipresent hypocrisy at the conservative core.

15. **Evolution.**
    - Republicans don't believe in evolution, just as they don't believe in any other science that disagrees with their rigid and unconforming sadistic and tribal world view, disproves their religion or merely makes them uncomfortable. Again, the poisonous influence of religion in politics is expressed in everything these people say and do. Were it not for religion, there would be absolutely no attempted justification for the conservatives' disbelief in the facts of evolution and indeed therefore the foundation of all biological science.

    - Progressives and independents do understand that evolution is real, because a literal planetful of science and evidence prove it is true. Every single scrap of evidence humans have observed since we developed brains and eyes have proven evolution to be incontrovertibly true. See "science", above.

24

16. **Stem Cell Research.**
    - Conservatives believe, for solely religious reasons, that this work is wrong. They seek to insert religious beliefs into law in violation of the Constitution and to legislate against this valuable research. No matter how many diseases could be cured, no matter how much misery could be prevented, no matter how many lives could be improved or saved, Republicans are opposed to this and many other lines of work that could actually improve human well-being. Their only justification for it is their ignorant, immoral and sadistic religion and mindless dogmatic groupthink.

    - Progressives and independents, for practical, ethical and moral reasons, know this and many other lines of research should be funded and strongly pursued, and they seek legislative support for them.

17. **Climate Change.**
    - The facts of climate change are denied by Republicans, understood and accepted by progressives and independents and also and more importantly, 97-99% of actual trained and experienced climate scientists and indeed the entire rest of the globe. Due to their susceptibility to tribalism, conspiracy theories, lies, religion and xenophobia, American conservatives actually believe they alone among all humans have the truth about this issue and the entire rest of humanity along with all related science is wrong.

    - Just as in all their other science denials and politico-religious claims, Republicans selectively pick and choose what science they want to believe in, and it is always and only the science that suits their particular religious, political and financial goals. Just as they pick and choose which bits of their allegedly divinely inspired or written holy book they live by and as they reject all the rest of their god's words, they pick and choose only the bits of science that they think support their goals. Which in this case means rejecting essentially the entire body of climate science. This is factually criminal, in that the impacts of climate change are guaranteed to damage and kill large numbers of people. Therefore through this specific isotope of antihuman and ignorant science denial they have deliberately chosen to bring about the suffering and death of large numbers of men, women and children.

- Like pretty much all other science these days except the kind that is needed to support the weapons, security and petrochemical industries, conservatives either do not believe in it, or just as in the long and disgusting line of coverups already uncovered in the tobacco, asbestos, sugar and oil industries, they know it is true but deliberately lie about it. Many of them also have the insane belief that the god they worship will not let the world be damaged in this way. Many more of them have the even more insane belief that their god is going to swoop back to the planet sometime really really soon – they promise! - and vacuum the godly up into some heavenly never-neverland, so they can damage the earth all they want until that time. See "science", above.

- Progressives and independents, not being ignorant, stupid, evil or insanely dogmatic, understand that science is the only actual method we have of discerning reality and of advising us on what to do about it. Therefore they work hard to solve the problem despite the lies, bibles, torches and pitchforks wielded by conservatives to block this progress.

18. **The Environment.**
   - Republicans don't believe that pollution and its impacts are real, or they do know this quite clearly but they just don't care. Both positions are contemptible and thoroughly immoral. They also

26

believe the only real evil is anything that impacts the quarterly earnings statement, their own power and paycheck or the business interests of their wealthy donors. They believe in their absolute Freedom to dump pollutants anywhere they like on the land or in our water, air and food, no matter how many people get horribly sick or die as a result. It is important to note that the GOP was not always so virulently anti-science and pro-pollution. It was no tree-hugging liberal but actually a Republican president, indeed the caustic and immoral Richard Nixon, who established the Environmental Protection Agency in 1970. The continued increases in insanity, immorality and sadism in the GOP since the late 1970s have been expressed in its actions to deliberately destroy the environment.

- Progressives and independents, using established science, understand the huge health and safety impacts of pollution and wish to take measures to keep it to a bare minimum. Progressives also know that they and everybody else on the planet have the Freedom to not be forced to or tricked into ingesting and inhaling toxic pollutants, carcinogens, petrochemicals and heavy metals in their air, food and water. See "climate change" and "science", above.

19. **Renewable Energy and Failed Conservo-Republican Dogma.**
    - Republicans and their actions embody the term "conservative", in two senses. One is that they are doggedly and blindly beholden to 'the way things are and the way things have always been'. No matter how foolish, unproductive or outdated something is, conservatives will cling to the childish mental security blanket of what they have always known and what they have always done, and often only an irresistible force from the outside will change this. Throughout history, conservatives have acted like

current Republicans and have been the ones who were violently against things like replacing horses with cars, going from boats with sails to those with engines, using aircraft, using medicine rather than prayer to treat disease, freeing slaves, letting women and black persons vote, and all the rest of history's examples of infantile fear of and dangerous hostility toward change and actual improvements in well-being.

- The other Republican problem in this area is their willingness to perpetrate evil up to and including killing people in their pursuit of the "IGM" end state. When a Republican reaches a position where money and power are flowing in, the *"I Got Mine"* mindset kicks in and they will be ruthless in their drive to keep that IGM status. They will lie, cheat, steal, obfuscate, attack and even kill to maintain it. They will work equally hard to "conserve" their own IGM status, no matter how many people are damaged by it. American politics and industry today are overflowing with examples of such brazen immorality and evil.

- Both of the above positions are contemptible and thoroughly immoral. Conservatives and Republicans cling to their positions with a death grip and can't even bear the thought of having to change from the path they have been on, even if that path clearly leads over a cliff. The herd animal sheeple mentality is the core of the conservative mindset.

- A perfect example demonstrating both of the above problems in one issue is the current and pending decline of petrochemical (generally coal but oil and gas will follow) extraction and the entrenched and immoral resistance to renewable energy. The coal, oil and gas worker is often a strong conservative and strongly embedded in and beholden to his job, and he basically does it just the way his pappy and his pappy's pappy and so on have done it back to when

Adam left the Garden of Eden with his pick and shovel and started digging coal. The mining company executives love having their drones get sick and die after preferably short careers of making lots of money for the executives without being able to draw either pension or health benefits. Changing to another industry would be a massive psychological challenge for both the worker and the executive, and like a gambler continuing to pull the lever on a slot machine, they will continue to pour money and effort into the machine until they are out of money.

- Conservatives, by their very nature and psychological weaknesses, fail to properly plan for and set the conditions for change. The executives will ride their businesses into bankruptcy and their workers into their grave, as long as they have extracted as much money as they can out of the businesses, the workers and their communities. The workers are happy to drone on into those graves. This paradigm is one of the most dangerous core problems with the conservative mindset, and it is rapaciously and evilly embodied in the GOP and its immoral and shortsighted practices.

- Progressives and independents, being students of history, economics, military history, and especially psychology and social and environmental science, and able to use reason to process all that data, know that change is essential to survival. Billions of years of evolution prove that if species don't change, they die. Thousands of years of human civilization prove that if businesses and cultures don't change, they die. Progressives know this and fight for, obviously, progress. Taking the petrochemical industry as an example, progressives know that petrochemicals are a finite resource. They know their use damages the people in the industries, damages the environment and continues to use up a nonrenewable resource.

They are working hard to build the renewables industry and to set the conditions for workers in the petrochemical industry to migrate to the renewables industry or some other field of work. This must be done using tax, investment, trade, education, retraining and other mechanisms. But even while progressives and independents are working hard to implement this badly needed process, conservatives block them whenever they can and however they can. Republicans are happy to let workers be fired or go without a job rather than taking some of the bloated wealth they have accrued and use it to help workers get job retraining and ease their transition to a new career field. This is the utter failure of the sadistic, rapacious and immoral Republican and conservative ethos.

20. **Crime and the Rule of Law.**

- Conservatives think the duly enacted law of the land only applies to them when it conforms to their beliefs of what is right and wrong, and when it enables them to persecute and prosecute their political, social and economic opponents. Conservatives today can be counted on to embody the worst and most craven hypocrisy when it comes to holding the guilty accountable. They scream loudly and endlessly about crimes committed by the poor, and they work to maximize punishments for these people while at the same time dismissing or ignoring massive amounts of white collar crime and ensuring that even when convicted, the white collar crime penalty is a slap on the wrist. Trump said it best, and it is probably the only thing he has said in his entire life that is wholly true – that he could shoot someone and not lose voters.[12] That he would say that, and that it is true of millions of his voters, says all that need be said about the GOP's disdain for the rule of law and their desire to punish the poor while protecting those in their tribe from that rule of law. It clearly shows their Satanic immorality. Conservatives embody the phrase 'the end justifies the means', regardless of whatever evil and/or hypocrisy this includes.

- Progressives and independents know that the rule of law applies all the time, to everyone, and especially to those in elected office due to their position in places of public trust. There are some exceptions, however, in the cases where some progressives seek amnesty for illegal immigration (see below) and the occasional empty-headed bleeding heartistry which seeks to inappropriately remove the blame for an act from the perpetrator.

21. **Immigration.**
- Conservatives want to expel Muslims, Mexicans and illegal immigrants, plus ban entry or immigration by Muslims and/or other groups they fear or don't like. This is patently foolish on too many levels to count, but it is a clear result of the terminally fearful, fragile and sadistic xenophobic conservative psychology. While it is true that an extremely large number of people who happen to practice Islam are no friends of the West, and it is also true that some would indeed conduct attacks of some kind if given the opportunity, there are large numbers of natural-born and white-as-snow Christian American citizens and legal non-Muslim immigrants who are right-wing domestic terrorists and/or criminals responsible for a large amount of crime in the US, to include murder. Much of the angst about immigration today is not founded on any factual basis except conservative xenophobia, tribalism and sadism.

- Progressives and independents are actually all over the map on this issue, from those who support the rule of law in all parts regarding immigration, to those who would have nearly open borders despite the law, to those who would abolish ICE. But they generally understand the rule of law always applies, so they seek a legal resolution for illegals already in the country and those who will enter illegally. What separates the conservative from the progressive is the conservative xenophobic tribalism and hatred for people not like themselves, and their highly easily triggered fear response. Progressives generally look to reason and compassion for policies involving human beings, and conservatives do not. Conservatives look to punishment and/or violence and harsh treatment as a first option while progressives look to stabilize the situation and understand the scope and root cause(s) of the problem. Some progressives and independents are so viscerally disgusted by seeing the US government deliberately put children in cages for the sadistic purpose of terrorizing people and deterring immigration that they over-react and seek to eliminate agencies rather than implement both appropriate law that provides for American security and a humane execution of that law.

22. **Crime and Immorality.**

- No single ethnic or religious group has a monopoly on illegal or evil acts, though atheists are statistically by far among the most law-abiding and moral people[13] in the US and across the world. If one looks hard enough, one can locate superlative citizens who are Muslim or Christian, and it is extraordinarily easy to name thoroughly evil people who profess their deep and sincere Christian faith either quietly or ostentatiously. In America today conservatives have hijacked religion and conflated it with morality and patriotism through aggressive and disingenuous media and legal actions. Yet it is the faithful and conservative Republicans who are by far the most criminal and immoral, from citizens to legislators to governors and presidents. Many types of crimes and immorality are statistically higher in red states, from violent crime to murder to rape. Even divorce, seen as immoral by many Christians, is higher in red states. Hate crimes, white nationalism, bigotry and misogyny are epidemic among Republicans, with a significant spike accompanying the rise of Trump and Pence and their sadistic xenophobia.

The GOP's base includes the KKK, white nationalists, conspiracy theorists, domestic terrorists and even foreign adversaries such as Vladimir Putin. Making all this much worse is that the GOP both deliberately chooses to ignore these facts and the root causes of the crime and immorality and also chooses to do nothing but increase rates of incarceration, which actually exacerbates the problem. The GOP's actions are increasing the rates of violent crime in the US and they refuse to accept this.

- Another seemingly intractable issue is that what Republicans believe to be immoral are only perceived by them to be such because of their sadistic faith-based ethos. From murdering alleged witches to supporting slavery to Prohibition to the endless hypocritical moralizing by today's religio-political Republican complex, conservatives throughout American history have always been and still are unceasingly fact-free in their ranting and thuggish sadistic words and deeds.

- Progressives and independents generally abide by the rule of law, have lower rates of crime and seek to use science and reason to identify the root causes of crime and immorality then work constructively to address them. Their reasonable and appropriate methods of problem solving are blocked at every turn by the mindless swarms of conservatives screaming about everybody else's alleged sin and immorality while hypocritically committing countless so-called "sins" and crimes themselves and deliberately not working to solve these problems. Conservatives in America are the source and enabler of much of the crime and immorality in this country.

23. Gun Control.

- Conservatives think gun control is an oxymoron, in the same way they view 'women's rights' as an oxymoron. They think that no matter how many guns there are on the streets or in classrooms or nurseries, many more of them is always much, much better. They believe no one should be denied the Freedom to pack as much heat as he can carry, completely regardless of the danger to others. In their unparalleled but typical gutless and immoral hypocrisy, however, elected Republicans are still universally spineless cowards and unabashed hypocrites, because they refuse to allow guns at their rallies or in their governmental chambers at the same time they are trying to fill middle schools, colleges and churches with them.

  And they are even so unsurpassably hypocritically and cravenly cowardly as to avoid holding town halls[14] because these gun-lovin' GOP snowflakes are pants-wettingly scared of their own constituents coming to their events with the guns they are trying to force into grade schools. Only in Republican politics and religion is such gobstopperingly evil immorality and hypocrisy on full and public display. Only in Republicanism is there such strident and cheerful acceptance of the collateral damage of heaps of murdered children and the unborn which result from their extremist and fundamentalist gun theology.

- Progressives and independents see the need for common sense gun control legislation and indeed a holistic approach to this issue intended to make people safe while still adhering to the Constitution. They know there is a path forward on the gun issue that doesn't include mass numbers of mass murders at high schools and grade schools and masses of small coffins filling the nation's graveyards.

- What is worse, and in acts of hypocrisy and Big Lie propagation that would put Orwell's Big Brother to shame, conservatives blame these bullet-ridden mass murders on mental health issues[15] yet at the same time are doing all they can to reduce health care for millions of Americans. They also have voted to repeal[16] sensible legislation that made it harder for people with significant mental illness to get guns. In other words, conservatives and Republicans are very deliberately making it as easy as possible for mass gun murderers to perpetrate those massacres, then they offer the contemptible 'thoughts and prayers' to the families of the slain, while the pools of children's blood coagulate on the floors of their classrooms.

  Conservatives with their Satanic forked tongues thus say that the blastocyst must be protected from harm at all costs, but once these cells have turned into thousands of men, women and children, they must live in a society which Republicans have deliberately made far more dangerous and unsafe. Such evil is truly a devil's masterpiece.

24. **Bigotry.**

- Conservatives, due to a combination of their upbringing and their own psychology, usually reinforced by the authoritarian and sadistic culture in which they are raised, are extremely strongly prone to out-group hostility, persecution, intolerance and bigotry in all forms. Conservative states, governors and legislators are using so-called 'religious freedom' as a disingenuous cover for many forms of blatant bigotry and discrimination. The GOP is an organization of bigots, and every day in America provides more and more proof of this.

- Progressive states don't make discriminatory laws, they don't gerrymander minorities and people of color out of voting power and they don't enact laws designed to remove the right to vote from conservatives or people with whom they disagree. Progressives strive for an inclusive society and while they may disagree with immorality and sadism, they still seek a pluralistic society, as our founding documents, our founding ethos, our original national motto and simple basic human decency call for. Conservatives have completely rejected the noble "from many, one" founding ethos of this country.

25. **Susceptibility to Bias.**

- Conservatives, again by the facts of their upbringing and psychology, are much more likely to believe exaggerations of reality or "alternative facts".[17] This means they believe bullshit to a ridiculous degree that actually can't be fully understood by sane, critical and rational thinkers. The exaggerations and assertions are not facts at all but are simply lies designed to scare and manipulate the listener. Conservatives are extraordinarily susceptible to manipulation, lies, fear and bigotry, and they are far more likely to act on these lies than are progressives and independents. This has been the case for millennia. Today's GOP is just the latest incarnation of history's anti-Semites, torch-and-pitchfork wielders, witch burners and fascist mobs led by the loudest and most hateful mouths.

- Progressives are by nature, and often also by nurture, more skeptical, reflective and analytical, particularly since they were not raised by people who dismiss or suppress critical thinking, as conservatives do. As a result, progressives and conservatives in America often cannot even agree on incontrovertible objective realities. This is perhaps the cornerstone of the entire failure to compromise, and the imbalance is tilted in one direction. Republicans will look at an incontrovertible fact and deny or twist it as much as they can in order for it to fit into their twisted politico-religious theology. Groups of humans cannot resolve differences when one side does not, will not, or perhaps even cannot, see reality.

26. Economic Systems, From Socialism to Capitalism.

- Conservatives jump to conclusions faster than a hyperactive flea on a hot plate overdosing on cocaine. Since they are unbelievably easily triggered, hypertribal, highly uniformed and strongly distrustful of reality that contradicts their feelings, having a factual discussion about this topic is very difficult. The fact is that America is already extremely socialistic, in the sense of publicly and communally funded services which all citizens receive, but conservatives deliberately ignore this or try to lie about it. A few of these services include:

  o Our Army, Navy, Air Force, Marine Corps and Coast Guard, including the active, reserve and National Guard components.
  o Our Border Patrol, the Department of Homeland Security, the FBI and the CIA.
  o Our Departments of Agriculture, Health and Human Services, Housing and Urban Development, Justice, Labor, State, Interior, Transportation and Veterans Affairs.
  o Our Environmental Protection Agency, the Food and Drug Administration and the Centers for Disease Control and Prevention.
  o Our police, fire and EMT services.
  o Social Security, Medicare, Medicaid and social services.
  o Our roads, bridges, waterways, tunnels, much of our water and other infrastructure.
  o Our national and state parks, libraries and monuments.
  o Much of our national science and technology capability, including our space program.
  o Our public schools.

- Conservatives continually scream about how the US will turn into a failed so-called "socialist" disaster overnight, "like Venezuela!", if a progressive is elected president. This is unbridled ignorant lies and idiocy. For one thing, the condition most pushing America toward failed banana republic status is the actions of Republicans and their corruption of everything from the rule of law to the courts to morality and ethics in government. For another thing, classical socialism in the sense of a total government takeover of every means of production and goods and services is absolutely not the goal of the vast majority of progressives. Only a few fringe nuts on the left who don't know or understand history or human nature want such a condition.

True full socialism and communism have a long history of failure for multiple reasons. Human psychology has not changed since these failures, so there is no reason to think the prior failures of these systems will be any different now or anytime until the human brain does change. Human psychology does not support living under full communism, full socialism or full capitalism. Normal humans fall on a spectrum in their individual drives and capacities, and normal human societies reflect the human characteristics of group cohesion, group support and reciprocal altruism. They also reflect a tit-for-tat redress of wrongdoings from criminal action to simple laziness and coat-tail riding. Nobody likes a freeloader.

A truly well-functioning and productive society will blend the good parts of capitalism with the good humanist socialistIC – emphasis on the "IC" - elements that maximize human well-being for all citizens. It will enable capitalism to function but the society must be heavily regulated to ensure that actions contrary to the well-being of the people are both prohibited and strongly punished.

In order to do that, Americans need to understand both the above facts of history and psychology and the fact that neither this country nor any sane and well-functioning country is founded on unbridled capitalism. America should never function like a sadistic oligarchy or dictatorship, as it does at every level when Republicans are in political power. America is a democratic republic that damn well does need to be more socialistIC - again with emphasis on the "IC" – than it is now.

And if conservatives want to stop being world-class blowhards and hypocrites, they need to make sure they don't work for any of these so-called socialistic organizations. So no conservative should *ever* work in any publicly-funded position at the city, state or federal level, to include the government and even the military, which is one of the most socialistic organizations in the entire USA, with its subsidized housing and other allowances plus its relatively flat pay scales. Conservatives will also need to lobby for legislation enabling them to voluntarily stop paying taxes for then be individually removed from the rolls of Social Security, Medicare, Medicaid and all other social services.

- Progressives, particularly Democrats, do a terrible job of communicating on this subject. While it is unfortunately true that 99.99% of conservatives don't do nuance at all, and they usually see things in childish black and white while not understanding the world is mostly in the gray space in between, and it is unfortunate that progressives have to dumb down their talking points and discussions to enable conservatives to understand them, this is just a fact of life.

Trying to discuss nuance and details with a conservative is like trying to tell Donald Trump about quantum physics. The conservative won't understand a word you are saying, what you are saying will likely go against all their ignorant and uninformed preconceptions and feelings, they will get mad and defensive about it, they will lash out at you for being arrogant and elitist, and they will start yelling at you and potentially become violent when you persist.

So yes, progressives and independents have to use baby talk and lower themselves to speak "conservativese". Use small words, short phrases and lots of pictures. Use very simple concepts and only one at a time. Get a good slogan catchphrase and repeat it often. You will have to scare them into shutting up and paying attention. Tell them you are going to take away all their guns, beat their god to death in public with a bunch of bibles, burn down their churches, enforce Mexican Sharia law on them, make their daughters marry nonwhite men and go to Muslim schools, prohibit white men from any jobs except picking strawberries and digging ditches and say you will make Hillary Clinton president for life.

Then, once you have their attention, and if you haven't been shot by one of these trigger-happy self-proclaimed god-fearin' Christians, you can start negotiating. You can ratchet back from the above positions and try to reach an appropriate middle ground which incorporates sensible and proven socialistIC and humanistic values and socio-economic policies. Take charge of the narrative. Show them places which are much more socialistic than the USA and show them how much better life will be if they just adopt some of the smart things those other countries do. Bring some citizens from those countries to the US and have them travel with progressive candidates, spreading the humanistic and socialistIC gospel. Particularly in the South, ensure these traveling socialistic evangelists are buxom and blonde, since breasts speak to conservative males far more than any brains or facts ever could. Above all,

> understand that conservatives are at their core
> frightened snowflakes desperately afraid of change.

The above is far from complete yet is quite a significant and important set of issues, and it reflects differences both cavernously broad and extremely deep on issues of extreme importance to most people. And the gaps aren't ones that can be papered over or lived with. Bigotry is unacceptable in all times and in all places, and should be called out and eliminated whenever it appears. Denial of the facts of science, economics and reality is not a position with which there can be ever any compromise whatsoever. There is not an acceptable degree of degradation or suppression of women, children, minorities or other groups. Education is not a means to institutionalize rote thinking and conformity to authority; it is the path to enlightenment, human progress and well-being.

Even on the topics where there could be compromise, conservatives don't want compromise. They want everything only their own way and they don't entertain discussion or give and take. Their position is one which was the way of life in certain parts of Europe in the Dark Ages and later in the 1930s and 1940s, and in autocracies and dictatorships throughout human history across the globe.

If you were a marriage counselor not hamstrung by the bizarre, immoral and antihuman rules of the Catholic cult, and a couple with such divergent and contradictory views came to your office for guidance, what would you advise them? "Oh, just focus on the most important issues and the others will take care of themselves?" Or "You need to find places where you can compromise, even though one of you is intractable and also denies reality and needs serious counseling, education and a major attitude adjustment."

Or would you say "You two are like matches and gasoline, as bad as Catholic and Protestant or Sunni and Shia or Catholic and Jew; how the hell did you two ever get together in the first place? Get drunk one night at a masquerade party then have a drive-through wedding before the alcohol wore off? Shotgun wedding after the rabbit died? This marriage is so far gone we need to get you far apart right now, before the shooting starts."

Splitting up a dysfunctional couple is relatively easy. Splitting up a country that has been established for over two centuries would not be easy. But if the need for an action is greater than the need for that action to be avoided, it can be done.

I have a modest proposal for how to implement the separation of the two warring camps in the United States in a cordial and fair manner. In a Solomonic nod to the biblical, the current United States of America would be split into two parts, like a glacier calving off a massive chunk of itself due to the climate change which conservatives deny is a real thing. The dividing line would roughly separate the current nation into northern and southern halves, along lines which to absolutely no one's surprise and for very obvious reasons, very closely parallels the dividing line between Civil War-era Confederate pro-slavery and Union anti-slavery states.

Figure 1 below indicates how these new additions to the global community of nations would look on a map. Following conventional American political color coding norms, the angry apoplectic red states to the south represent the future home of those rough and tumble, self-reliant, 'git'er done', Bible thumpin', gun totin', school voucher likin', plain talkin', Confederate flag wavin', Mexican hatin' and Confederate statue worshipin' so-called "Real American" conservatives.

The calmer blue states to the north represent the new home for the contemplative, more social, mutually supportive and Enlightenment-style educated and rational progressives who use facts and reality as a basis for decisions and policy.

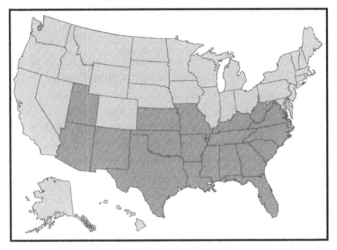

Figure 1. A Modest Proposal For A Post-United States Political Arrangement.

Higher education, science and art are anathema to the conservative core missions of indoctrination, keeping the white race pure as the driven snow, maintaining constant wars, denying scientific realities, oppressing and expelling out-groups, stratifying society and above all, making money for the top 1% and ensuring their extremist, fascistic and oligarchical vision of Freedom at all costs. Anything that does not maximize the efficiency of the society to achieve these goals would not be welcome anyway.

Therefore, the north will keep Stanford, MIT, the Ivy League and Northwestern, while divesting of BYU, Oral Roberts, Bob Jones and Liberty "Universities". They will keep the Smithsonian, the Field Museum and the Shedd Aquarium while divesting of the Creation Museum, the Ark Encounter and the Confederate Museums (yes, plural). They will keep Fallingwater and the Guggenheim, while washing their hands of the Mormon Tabernacle and the Lakewood Megachurch.

All schools in the new Red Land could be religiously based, teaching only the purest forms of biblical creationism and literalism, unquestioned religious dogma and the full suppression of critical thought. All that need be taught beyond that baseline would be the most basic and rudimentary skills necessary to provide an uncritical and compliant supply of millions of uneducated and highly propagandized Soviet Union-style drones well-suited for their lives in below-minimum-wage jobs with few or no benefits.

This would enable the maximum efficiency of the State by empowering the blessed Job Creators, profit be upon them, with the Freedom to set working conditions, wages and jobs at the absolute bare minimum level deemed appropriate to barely sustain the drones' physical existence while hypermaximizing profits for the most holy corporations and the super-wealthy.

This process is actually already well underway, as reflected in red state policies across the US, Republican federal policy and the following paragraphs. The new blue nation can keep blathering on about how so-called 'higher education' is important, but that sort of crazy talk just won't work in a red State focused on war, profits and persecution of minorities, not things as useless, and as dangerous, as higher education and independent thinking.

Red Land is already moving far down the path toward deliberately institutionalized ignorance, as shown in Figure 2 below, which is a graphic depiction of composite ACT scores[18] from 2016, by state. It clearly shows Red Land states, particularly those in the Southeast, to be well behind many Blue Land states.

With full implementation of charter schools and the blending of church and state, Red Land could one day drive all of its states' composite scores below 20, not just half of them. And the ones under 20 could shoot for 15! That would really make the masters happy.

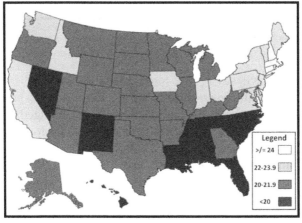

Figure 2. 2016 US ACT Composite Scores By State.

Figure 3 below is an extremely illuminating graphic which was seen for months following the presidential election. It is the 2016 Electoral College map.[19]

Note the strong correlation between those states which went for Trump and those with the lowest ACT scores. One could almost say that the more ignorant a state is, the more it went for Trump.

Figure 3. Map Reflecting Electoral College Votes by State (Clinton in Light Gray and Trump in Dark Gray).

OK, I will say it. The most ignorant states, that is the states with the worst-performing ACT testers, with likely similarly academically and intellectually-challenged or lower-performing parents and grandparents, perform just as poorly in the voting booth as they do in the classroom. Stupid is as stupid does, as the saying goes.

So Texas can put its oil money where its holier-than-thou mouth is and lead a motley group of red states in forming a new Promised Land, indeed a land which they can reshape in their own image. They could even fall to their unworthy and penitent knees and breathlessly proclaim it a 'born again' nation. It would be blessedly free of pesky laws, regulations and progressives.

Conservatives from north of the new border could migrate south to the new lebensraum[20], making a permanent pilgrimage to the newly risen holy land. They could settle in any of the former states of Texas, Oklahoma, Kansas, Arizona, New Mexico, Utah, Louisiana, Arkansas, Missouri, Mississippi, Alabama, Georgia, Tennessee, Kentucky, Florida, South Carolina, North Carolina, Virginia or West Virginia.

The names, absolutely unsurprisingly, roll off the tongue like a recitation of historic Civil War battleground sites. And in the full spirit of segregating these southern red states from those to the north, they could reclaim the Confederate heritage fetish they love so much and merge it with their current attitudes and declare themselves sanctuary states for discrimination, bigotry and antipathy toward science and nonwhite people.

Surely those on the conservative side of the political divide, who despise progressives so much, would see the greater good in such a construct. The possibilities are truly endless, and for a group of people who are instinctively very xenophobic and compulsively nationalistic, having an enclave of a great many millions of people just like them would be a paradise, indeed almost a heaven, on earth.

Imagine the possibilities! Think about what could happen with having totally free rein for all the right-wing talking points which conservatives have been bleating about for years, finally and completely unencumbered by soft-headed progressive resistance and enabled by a fully complicit population and government at all levels.

Their self-professed status as the only people who know how to 'do' immigration right would enable them to take full charge of that 'big, beautiful wall' on the border, and indeed they could take on practically the entire Mexican border security mission. No arguing with progressives about making the wall or how many heaped hundreds of billions it would cost. No arguing about how to so-called 'legally' arrest, deport or shoot trespassers. When Freedom is at stake, no cost would be too high and no action too drastic.

They can at last get rid of that pesky secular Constitution and its annoying wall between church and state, and gleefully erect statues and posters and banners (oh my) of whichever version of the Ten Commandments they most like on publicly funded or government property anywhere at all. Ostentatious displays of the official religion could crop up like weeds after a heavy rain and not only would no one protest, the creation of a theocracy would be met with many hallelujas and much rejoicing. Public stonings, hangings, burning of witches and disobedient children and full biblical sadism could finally be implemented!

And there would be no need to keep lying about religious freedom not actually being a contrived cover for trying to legislate the deliberate discrimination and persecution of fellow human beings. Every single citizen would have the Freedom to practice his or her own individual principles of religious freedom and bigotry against anyone else in the entire country without worries about progressives and their damn Yankee secular Constitution.

There would be no need to keep trying to sneak creationism and religion into public schools and the government sphere inside the Trojan Horse of 'intelligent design' or any of its mutations or derivatives. Religion could be a part of not only every school's basic curriculum, but actually part of every subject. History could be rewritten to not only show how Jesus inspired everything good in history and how Satan himself caused everything bad, but that history itself only began about six thousand years ago. Math would be performed in the light of the perfect holy equations, the everlasting and unchangeable fact that two plus two equals four everywhere on earth being hailed as undeniable proof of Jesus's existence.

Science textbooks could be rewritten to eliminate such ungodly and biblically confounding unpleasantries as evolution, natural selection, astronomy, cosmology, geology, geomorphology, limnology, hydrology, climatology, paleoclimatology, physics, chemistry, genetics, archaeology, neuroscience, botany, anatomy, cell biology, medicine, ecology, evolutionary biology, immunology, microbiology, paleontology, zoology, psychology, biopsychology, and indeed any other field of science that conflicts with a biblically-based interpretation of the world.

The only problem would arise when the Protestants and the Catholics would have to take time out from warring with each other and with the Mormons for top Christian billing in the schools to suppress any crazy Muslims, Hindus, Buddhists, Shintos, Jews, Sikhs, Folk religionists, pagans, Jains, Cargo Cultists or adherents of the other 4000-odd religions still extant who tried to use this unfettered religious Freedom to get equal time in the Red Land classroom and government for *their* religious beliefs and histories.

And don't even spare a thought for the nonreligious who couldn't escape Red Land; they'd be so far underground they'd be closer to China than Alabama. Since any such people would already have had to be crazy to want to live in a Christian State religiofascist theo/thugocracy in the first place, suppression and persecution then arrest and deportation or execution of these groups would surely be appropriate for the continued moral and social health of the nation and its impressionable youth, who could of course only be truly and appropriately moral citizens if forcibly taught unadulterated biblically-literal Christianity.

They wouldn't have to try to come up with so many different ways to deprive minorities or poor people out of civic or societal relevance, or indeed to even allow them to vote at all. And just like the non-Christians, any sass or backtalk from these people and it would be 'over the big beautiful wall' with them.

They could immediately form new diocese/parish state governments and a whole new national government and run them without any kind of EPA meddlin'. They could instantly free their economy from the crippling weight of having to preserve the environment for current and future generations. They could tear down the entire environmental oversight process and unleash the raw and unadulterated power of unregulated industry to frack, pollute and ravage at will. Drill, baby, drill! Frack, baby, frack! Dump, baby, dump!

No more scrubbers on smoke stacks. No more busybody EPA agents coming around like sneaky 'revenooers' handing out fines for such unimportant things as dumping poison in rivers or allowing lead, mercury or arsenic into drinking water. No limits on heavy metals or other toxins in the water, the air or the soil. Freedom!

And no fripperies like lawsuits from disease, premature death and birth defects, tap water that glows or that you can set on fire, because Freedom is more important than such transient things as health when there is money to be made.

Oil and gas can reclaim their rightful place as the King and Queen of Energy. No nancypants liberal green-energy nonsense would even be allowed in the country. It could even be made illegal, indeed it would be considered immoral, to possess information about such subversive evils. And Rick Perry wouldn't have to look at the sign on his door to remember which Department he wanted to get rid of, because the former Department of Energy could be changed to the Department of Oil. Now there's a name no self-respectin' Texan would *ever* forget.

And of course, what would a truly conservative new nation need with an IRS? Finally the flat tax can become a reality, and people at the bottom of the income ladder will finally have to pay into the system, just like the put-upon millionaires and billionaires have had to *so unfairly* do for so long. Finally conservative tax policies would have full sway, with preferential treatment in the new rules and laws naturally going to the largest campaign contributors.

Then, after a few disastrous years of draconian and short-sighted conservative tax policy failure, since Louisiana would be deeply embedded in the heart of the new country, the new central government could rely on certain shadowy denizens of that highly idiosyncratic state to join with lawmakers to try to conjure a working version of actual voodoo economics which would magically create out of thin air the massive amounts of revenue that would be needed to cover the cavernous fiscal gaps blasted open by the tax policy.

And they can have a war whenever and wherever they want, with no pissing and moaning by limp-wristed State Departments (sad!) or advice by pointy-headed political and military scientists and historians. No more hawks fighting with doves in the halls of Congress, no discussions about resolutions or coalitions or how much it might cost, no worries about what might come after the war, no need to get anything as namby-pamby as 'consensus' before whipping out the military and carpet bombing and mini-gunning the target *de jure* to their tiny hearts' content.

Hell, they can have a War of the Week, every week, if they wanted to. That would actually be better than what they've been doing, with the same damn war dragging on for year after year after year, and the general population losing track of and interest in how many people are losing limbs or dying. A War of the Week would keep the public's short attention span from wandering. In the age of Fox and Trump, it could even be a TV event, fully televised and with prizes for the citizens who correctly guessed the next target. Or it could tie in to a new 'reality TV' show, maybe titled "Celebrity Confederate", since so there are so many of them in elected office.

And no Supreme Court, less'n it's one with no empty-headed libtards on it. So if there's no libtards around who would be on a Supreme Court but true red-blooded conservatives? And if everybody thinks the same way, why would you need so many justices? Wouldn't just three do? Or maybe it would be best to have just one, since going from nine to one means you can shrink the government down by, well at least a few hunnert percent, right? And since one is better than nine, wouldn't none be better than one? Small government and all, you know. Couldn't you give the job of the Supreme Court to someone who already has a job? Now *that's* a good idea. But who?

Well, the President would be a great choice, since he's already got a job, and is supposed to know what's going on. In the extremely simple words of that monumentally simplest of conservatives, Bush the Lesser, he can be the Decider. So there you go. Conservatives like to be told what to do, they like strongmen, they say they don't like big government, and they say they pride themselves on efficiency. So the President will serve as judge, jury and Decider.

And of course since this will be a strongly and devoutly conservative theocracy, no government or governmental official at any level would ever be engaged in so much as a whiff of corruption, double dealing, alternative facts, spin, bribes, threats, intimidation, blackmail, nepotism, gangsterism or treason, as has been the case in such nations throughout history, the Decider would probably never have to do much anyway.

Red Land's rising coastal sea waters, caused of course by something besides "That Which Must Not Be Mentioned"[21], could theoretically eventually be perceived as a problem when hundreds of thousands of square miles of coastland become inundated under progressively more seawater. But not to worry! The well-heeled will have long since sold any such vulnerable land to willing and gullible uneducated drones, who were assiduously kept in the dark about the problem through public proclamations and carefully crafted charter school curricula and official propaganda and fatwas against the lies from the softies to the North and indeed from the entire rest of the world.[22] The drones living in the newly swamped areas might at some point realize they have a problem when the seawater started lapping at their front doors. But again, not to worry! There is a simple solution.

People in the South love fishing, and if there is more water and less land, then there's more places to go fishing! Look at what bounty the good lord has brought – not loaves, ok, but plenty of fishes! And when the slightly less dense among the drones begin to protest, they can be silenced with the eternal and unanswerable rejoinder of "Oh, well, god did it, what can you do? Nobody could have seen this magical sea level rise coming. He works in mysterious ways, and if you're having a problem, either it's your fault for being a rotten sinner or he's just testing your faith, so shut up and go back to sandbagging. Can't you see we're busy trying to win a war?"

Women and children can be put in their proper places, which is to say, respectively, barefoot, pregnant and compliant, and respectful and quiet except when spoken to. No abortions, no contraception, no exceptions. No Planned Parenthood, and no unnecessary medical procedures and wasted expenses on "women's" problems, whatever those are. Ever since Eve, women have *been* the problem, anyway. So screw 'em, both literally and figuratively, since that is every Red Land man's biblically derived prerogative.

And in this new Holy Red Land, with the ins and outs of the moving parts of the body politic machine suitably lubricated by fully god-approved biblical sexual practices, the men can reach back into those pages and renew polygamy and the keeping of concubines! What a deal! At least for rich men, that is. Red Land drones, bereft of much of anything else of worldly value, need not be left out. They too can engage in the Freedom to exercise their god-given Rights to exercise their sincerely held religious beliefs and earn a dime at the same time. They can engage in a thriving trade in selling their daughters to rich men as concubines, in full accordance with the biblical social model.

These rich men can then populate their harems and even trade concubines amongst each other when they get tired of the same old young women to sexually assault. They can take those bibles and MAPA - Make America Polygamous ASAP!

There could finally be an end to all the death and destruction which hurricanes, tornadoes, droughts and floods have wrought for so long throughout the bible belt. Finally, with all the gays, atheists and progressives having escaped or been thrown in cages or deported to the north or shot, and everybody in Red Land prayin' up a storm, surely their deity would see how Red Land had cleansed itself of these offensive vermin, and would take divine action to permanently shield them from all bad weather and send it either to the bad hombres down in Mexico or the socialist commie loser pinko multicultural politically correct heathens up north. So, no need for a FEMA either, whether it would be capable of 'doin' a heckuva job, Brownie'[23] or not.

And instead of being a shamelessly fact-free propaganda platform for the conservative and fact-free far right but have to lie about it, Fox News could relocate its HQ to Alabama or Mississippi or wherever the Red Land capital building would be, set up shop inside the president's office, run up a disciple's dozen Confederate flags up outside the building, incorporate the stars and bars into a new Fox logo, project hundred-foot-tall images of Ronald Reagan, Donald Trump, Roger Ailes, Bill O'Reilly and Vladimir Putin on the sides of the building, and once and for all finally drop the pretenses and operate openly in its mission to be a self-professed and blatantly unapologetic ~~lying shill~~ communications outlet for the conservative government.

But some might protest that Alaska and Hawaii both went to the north in the split, and that it was unfair. This is the right decision for some simple reasons. It is true that there is oil in Alaska so Red Land will want it very badly, but that's kind of the point. Keeping that oil in the ground will help keep ~~climate change~~ this warming trend which may or may not be real, or if it is some god's judgment for sin, from going out of control.

Since Republicans prefer their women to be barefoot and pregnant, and they have no tolerance for abortion or birth control, if Alaska went Red the conservative lily white Anglo population of the state would skyrocket. They would thus be a threat both to the native populations and also to the Canadians, who'd not be too happy to see another aggressive theocracy on yet another border after the first one relocated to the south.

Since rising sea water and continuous warming of more polar latitudes as a result of ~~climate change~~ things we can never know the truth about is likely to badly

56

damage the climate of Alaska, the native population will not be happy with those who did it, which would be likely to precipitate a conflict between the indigenous population and the willful perpetrators, with likely results the same as countless previous similar encounters in history. And one decimation of an indigenous population on the continent by Anglos is truly enough, so Alaska will need to go blue.

As for Hawaii, this really doesn't even pass the common sense test. There's no oil there and it's chock full of people who aren't white. Why would any Republican want any part of it? So it already cedes to Blue Land by default. Not to mention when sea level rises by a few feet, places like Waikiki will be inhabited by fish rather than tourists, so only left-leaning ecophiles would see the appeal of those areas. Besides, conservatives don't believe in volcano research.[24]

So in this new self-contained right wing 'island universe' echo chamber new nation, conservatives can have absolutely everything their own way. No IRS. No EPA. No FEMA. No SEC (free translation for all those living in the deep south - that's the Securities and Exchange Commission, and it don't got nuttin' to do wit' football). No Departments of State, Commerce, Interior, Education, Energy or any other useless wastes of time and money. They could cut down to just Defense, Oil and Homeland Security, with a dash of greatly expanded Coast Guard and Border Patrol, and shrink everything else to a bare minimum, or shift all these burdens to the state level.

The country would be a solidly lockstep bastion of true limitless conservative Freedom. Red Land would have nothing but unregulated industry, unlimited fracking, drilling at will, no limits on water or air or ground pollution, full wage suppression and no unprofitable nonsense like benefits for workers. There would be mandatory and biblically literal Christian prayer in all schools and workplaces, absolute denial of science and evolution, omnipresent religious and social bigotry and persecution and a church, jail and gallows on every street corner. There would be a gun in the hand of every schoolchild and open and concealed carry everywhere. There would be stoning of abortionists, atheists and disobedient children, immediate expulsion of Muslims, immigrants and minorities, all women and children quiet and subjugated, plus any other Wild Westisms and Old Testamentisms that sound good.

And finally, *finally*, they would be free of the shackles and chains that come with unwarranted charity and the dependence it fosters. There would be an end to all of the red state welfare that had been so evilly doled out to them by the former Uncle Sugar, because those rugged conservative individualists who hate government handouts so badly are unquestionably more than fully capable of managing their affairs when all federal government aid gets cut off. So no official government Ponzi schemes like Social Security and Medicare, they don't need none of that claptrap.

Finally the nation can stand on its own two feet and every man, woman and child can know they would never need to depend on the gubmint for *anythin'*, ever again. Mississippi, New Mexico, Alabama, Louisiana and Tennessee can stop being the five states that are currently the most dependent on government assistance[25], and can doggone well fend for themselves, like a real Red State should.

In their new Wild West, conservatives can set up a fully dog-eat dog, every-man-for-himself, Wild West-style, no-regulations capitalist system. They can stop paying them dang taxes and develop an alternate system more suited to the *Real American* way! They can all start paying protection money to some gang of local mercenaries in lieu of police protection. They can hire private corporations at appropriately high rates for fire and EMT services. Instead of them pesky taxes they can just pay a toll every single time they use a sidewalk, road, bridge or other corporately-owned transportation surface. If they still want to have such namby-pamby things as state and national parks, libraries or monuments, they will dang well happily pay several times what Blue Land people pay for an entry fee into theirs.

They will be rough and tough bootstrappers and gladly pay much higher tuition, fees and other costs to send their kids to unregulated and unmonitored religious charter schools and universities, now that all the public schools and public funding plus them pesky "edumacation standard" fripperies are gone.

Despite all the above newly-gained ability to pay for just the services they want, though, they will still have to pay for all the hyperactive armed forces, Border Patrol, Fascist Youth, Neighborhood Anti-Commie / Anti-Socialist / Anti-Liberal Safety Patrols and the state and federal secret police like the German Stasi and the Soviet Commissariat for Internal Affairs (NKVD). They will also have to fund the 50-foot tall Wall of Freedom around the entire country, the massively increased numbers of jails and the newly constructed concentration camps and gulags, which all states like this have to have.

Rather than taxes, Red Land could still collect the funding from the population but call it "Freedom Fees".

A conservative could call all this only one thing – not the Second Coming, maybe, but surely heaven on earth!

In fact it's highly likely that very conservative males reading this will have already had to change their underwear due to their inability to control their orgasmic arousal at contemplating such an arrangement. Their only question will be "When can we do it!!??"

The process of dissolution could be called Crexit, for ~~Crazies~~ Conservatives Exit. Catchy.

At end state, following a successful division of assets, some migration and voluntary resettlements of persons either to the north or to the south, and a formal declaration of the two new nations both on paper and on the ground, the new arrangement would be set. The new political strata from south to north would thus begin with a narcostate corruptocracy in Mexico, overlain by a brand new religiofascist theocratic corporation-state Red Land, then a tightly knit democracy or democratic republic Blue Land, and finally calm and no-changes no-drama Canada as the cherry or maple leaf on top.

But what to name the two brand-new nations? The blue nation would no doubt pick some fancy pantsy artsy fartsy name inspired by the Romans or the Greeks or somebody else with too much education who's been dead for a thousand years. And who would care, anyway? Progressives don't go around always having to thump their chests and talk about how wonderful they are, like conservatives do. One thing they wouldn't allow, though, would be for the Reds to usurp the name of the former United States of America. And since Red Staters also wouldn't let anyone else use the name, it would have to be circular-filed and retired as a national designation. Call it a mutually liquidated asset.

No, the real trick would be naming the new Red State. What should one call this new bastion of unfettered, "Real American" conservatism and ultimate Freedom? Since it would be the hardcore conservatives' hottest and wettest wet dream ever to live in a country that was 'all about them, all the time', the name would have to incorporate some flavor of the conservative ethos, plus have plenty of consonants to make it sound rough and tough. And it would need to sound like a place nobody would want to either go to or mess with, a place where just the *sound* of the name puts one off. It would have to instantly call to mind the impression of a nation with many people of a single mind, bound by mindless and unshakeable ideology and extremely strong faith, unmoved and indeed unmovable by unwelcome facts or influences.

There is actually a perfect name for this new nation, a name that would instantly reflect the perfect impression in all who heard it of exactly the kind of people who would want to live there.

I have another modest proposal, this time for the name of this new nation.

Conservastan.

It is truly the perfect name.

It's only one word long, so it is easy for the simple and uneducated drones who would live there to memorize, even though it has more than two syllables.

It has lots of consonants and sounds very manly and uncompromising.

It begins with "Conserva" which of course instantly conveys the whole point behind a Conservative nation.

It ends with 'stan', which instantly calls to mind a backward and corrupt nation filled with deeply religious and uneducated intolerant zealots who every day fall one more step behind the rest of the world in true humanistic morality, the rule of law and equality, education, fairness and opportunity for all people.

It reflects the unquenchable Republican penchant for continuous military action in the Middle East.

It conveys the theocratic overtones of the various current FuckedUpistans with the "Conserva" Fox News branding on the front end. It is perfect.

I hereby bring the motion to the floor.

Do I hear a second?

Bonus Points!!

Every country has to have a flag. The design below reflects the core values of Red Land, with iconography drawn from the inspirations and motivations of its founders and rabid supporters.

The MAGAFLAG™ will replace the Stars and Stripes as the symbol of a new, proud, aggressive, nationalistic, religiofascist theocratic corporation-state which won't listen to anyone, ever! Not even Jesus![26] It will fly high over the land, serving as a warning to the rest of the world of the itchy trigger fingers of its inhabitants and its utter resistance to the invasion of unwelcome information and ideas from the outside world. Not to mention a national embodiment of the Dunning-Kruger effect.

The Flag of Conservastan

The "MAGAFLAG", for when the Old South rises again, like a stinking zombie bent on death, pestilence and the destruction of civil society

In the new Christian State theocracy, the Crusaders prepare for battle against the dangerous progressives and Canadians up north

They see Israel as a soul brother and partner in war and End Times craziness no matter how long it takes

They see Russia as an a shining city on a hill, glowing with the light of Chernobyl and governed with a poisoned iron fist

Only lower in importance than the cross, the bible and "The Wall", the sacred gun is held in the greatest esteem and protects against all the bad hombres south of the border.

The blue diagonal "X" is a warning to everyone to stay the hell out and is a reminder of the Sacred Wall of Separation from them and everyone else. If anyone tries to come in they will criss-cross your body with star-tipped "bullets of freedom".

About The Author

Max Humana is a retired US military servicemember who still supports and defends the Constitution against all enemies both foreign and domestic through writing on the never-safe subjects of religion, politics, morality, humanity, truth and reason.

He is working to advance human knowledge and to rid the world of ignorance, stupidity and evil, and wants you to do the same.

References

1. Article on Time.com titled "The Party of No: New Details on the GOP Plot to Obstruct Obama", describing the GOP's entrenched and total opposition to every Obama position and action. Article by Michael Grunwald, 23 August 2012. Web resource at http://swampland.time.com/2012/08/23/the-party-of-no-new-details-on-the-gop-plot-to-obstruct-obama/

2. Article in *The Washington Post* online, titled "*Republicans had it in for Obama before Day 1*", discussing the wholly partisan anti-American actions by the GOP in Congress to stonewall Obama actions at all cost. Written by Jonathan Capehart, 10 August 2012. Web resource at https://www.washingtonpost.com/blogs/post-partisan/post/republicans-had-it-in-for-obama-before-day-1/2012/08/10/0c96c7c8-e31f-11e1-ae7f-d2a13e249eb2_blog.html

3. Article in *The New York Times* online, titled "*A Brief History of Deadly Attacks on Abortion Providers*", discussing some of the history of murders of abortion providers by people inspired by religio-conservative positions. Written by Liam Stack, 29 November 2015. Web resource at https://www.nytimes.com/interactive/2015/11/29/us/30abortion-clinic-violence.html

4. Article in *The New York Times* online, titled "*F.B.I. Investigating Kansas Shooting of Indian Men as Hate Crime*", describing the investigation of Trump and right-wing bigotry-inspired murder of one Indian man and the shooting of another as a hate crime. Written by Liam Stack, 28 February 2017. Web resource at https://www.nytimes.com/2017/02/28/us/kansas-shooting-indians-fbi.html?_r=0

5. Record of testimony of Dale L. Watson, the Executive Assistant Director, Counterterrorism / Counterintelligence Division of the FBI, to the Senate Select Committee on Intelligence, 6 February 2002. Testimony describes the danger and scope of domestic terrorism in the USA. The problem is still a massive one and has dangerously heightened in the Trump era. Web resource at https://archives.fbi.gov/archives/news/testimony/the-terrorist-threat-confronting-the-united-states

6. Article in *Newsweek* online, titled "*Right-Wing Extremists Are a Bigger Threat to America Than ISIS*", describing the extremely disturbing spread and scope of this massive problem. Written by Kurt Eichenwald, 4 February 2016. Web resource at https://www.newsweek.com/2016/02/12/right-wing-extremists-militants-bigger-threat-america-isis-jihadists-422743.html

7. Article in *Psychology Today* online titled "' Misinformation and Facts about Secularism and Religion", written by David Niose, 30 March 2011. Web resource at https://www.psychologytoday.com/us/blog/our-humanity-naturally/201103/misinformation-and-facts-about-secularism-and-religion

8. The 2012 Republican Party Of Texas Report of Platform Committee, which is a list of thoroughly antihuman, hypocritical, disingenuous, bigoted, anti-scientific and anti-intellectual religio-fascistic insanity. Web resource at http://s3.amazonaws.com/texasgop_pre/assets/original/2012Platform_Final.pdf

9. Article on *The Austin Chronicle* online titled "GOP Opposes Critical Thinking; Party platform paints original ideas as a liberal conspiracy", describing the full-blown anti-intellectualism of both the state and national GOP. Article by Richard Whitaker, 27 June 2012. Web

resource at
https://www.austinchronicle.com/daily/news/2012-06-27/gop-opposes-critical-thinking/

10. Publication from the National Education Policy Center titled "*NEPC Review: Separating Fact & Fiction: What You Need to Know About Charter Schools*", describing many of the lies told by the supporters and religiously-inspired backers of charter schools about those "schools". Document reviewed by NEPC staff members Gary Miron, William J. Mathis and Kevin G. Welner. Published 23 February 2015. Web resource at https://nepc.colorado.edu/thinktank/review-separating-fact-and-fiction

11. Article on the *Independent* online titled "Brazil rocked by abortion for 9-year-old rape victim", describing how the Vatican supported the excommunication of the mother and physicians who performed an abortion on this young innocent rape victim, but of course did not excommunicate the stepfather who raped the girl. This is classic GOP-type thinking, and it is fully biblically inspired, as are most GOP actions. Article by Guy Adams, 9 March 2009. Web resource at https://www.independent.co.uk/news/world/americas/brazil-rocked-by-abortion-for-9-year-old-rape-victim-1640165.html

12. Video clip on YouTube of Trump saying that he could shoot someone and not lose voters. Rather than merely being true on its face, which it surely is given the immoral and evil nature of his fascistic supporters, such an act would actually gain him stronger support among his Republican and conservative base. Web resource at https://www.youtube.com/watch?v=iTACH1eVIaA

13. Article on the *Friendly Atheist* online titled "What Percentage of Prisoners are Atheists? It's a Lot Smaller Than We Ever Imagined", citing data from the Federal Bureau of Prisons showing that atheists make up a tiny

percentage of the prison population as opposed to the masses of religious believers who are behind bars. Article by Hemant Mehta, 16 July 2013. Web resource at https://friendlyatheist.patheos.com/2013/07/16/what-percentage-of-prisoners-are-atheists-its-a-lot-smaller-than-we-ever-imagined/

14. Article on CNN.com titled "GOP lawmaker invokes Gabby Giffords in concerns about town hall safety", exposing the utter gutlessness and hypocrisy of the GOP on the subject of guns. Article by Eugene Scott, 23 February 2017. Web resource at https://www.cnn.com/2017/02/23/politics/louie-gohmert-gabby-giffords/

15. Article on *Slate* online titled "Trump Blames Shooting on "Mental Health," a Policy Area He Is Also Actively Undermining", exposing yet more foundational and thoroughly immoral GOP lies and hypocrisy. Written by Eleanor Cummins, 6 November 2017. Web resource at https://slate.com/technology/2017/11/trump-blames-texas-shooting-on-mental-health-but-is-limiting-access-to-care.html

16. Article on Vox.com titled "Yes, Congress did repeal a rule that made it harder for people with mental illness to buy a gun", describing more GOP anti-American craven lunacy and immorality. Written by German Lopez, 3 October 2017. Web resource at https://www.vox.com/policy-and-politics/2017/2/3/14496774/congress-guns-mental-illness

17. Article on *The Washington Post* online titled "Why conservatives might be more likely to fall for fake news", describing some of the body of research showing that conservatives tend not to critically analyze information from their in-group or if it supports their preconceptions. Article by Christopher Ingraham, 7 December 2016. Web resource at https://www.washingtonpost.com/news/wonk/wp/2016/12

/07/why-conservatives-might-be-more-likely-to-fall-for-fake-news/?utm_term=.55dbfc9e6899

18. Document from ACT.org showing ACT scores by state in the USA in 2016. Web resource at https://www.act.org/content/dam/act/unsecured/document s/CCCR-2016-Average-Scores-by-State.pdf

19. Article on Foxnews.com showing the results of the 2016 election. Web resource at https://www.foxnews.com/politics/elections/2016/preside ntial-election-headquarters

20. Article on The United States Holocaust Memorial Museum website titled "Lebensraum". The site noted that "The concept of Lebensraum—or "living space"—served as a critical component in the Nazi worldview that drove both its military conquests and racial policy." Republicans in America are ideologically aligned with aggressive fascism and are spirit brothers and sisters with the supporters of the Fourth Reich, thus this term is relevant. Web resource at https://encyclopedia.ushmm.org/content/en/article/lebensr aum

21. Article on *The Miami Herald* online titled "In Florida, officials ban term 'climate change'", describing how elected Republicans deliberately use their office to suppress science and truth, through the Big Brother / Big Lie banning of the terms "climate change" and "global warming" in official publications. Conservatives actually order scientists to not talk about science if it offends or disagrees with their donors or religio-political theology. Article by Tristram Korten, 8 March, 2015. Web resource at https://www.miamiherald.com/news/state/florida/article12 983720.html

22. Article on *The Guardian* online titled "Pew survey: Republicans are rejecting reality on climate change",

reflecting that most American Republicans deliberately and ignorantly reject science when it offends or disagrees with their donors or religio-political theology. Article by Dana Nuccitelli, 6 October 2016. Web resource at https://www.theguardian.com/environment/climate-consensus-97-per-cent/2016/oct/06/pew-survey-republicans-are-rejecting-reality-on-climate-change

23. Article at *USATODAY.com* titled "Hurricane Katrina's 'Brownie': Where is he now?", describing how George W. Bush told his then-FEMA chief how wonderful a job he was doing, despite it being likely the worst major disaster response in US history up to that point. Article by Matthew Diebel, 28 August, 2015. Web resource at https://www.usatoday.com/story/news/2015/08/28/katrinas-heckuva-job-brownie-where--he-now/32485703/

24. Article at NPR.com titled "Jindal Comment On Volcano Monitoring Causes Some To Erupt", describing yet another anti-science Republican's public idiocy as then-Louisiana Governor Bobby Jindal went on prime time television to criticize volcano research funding, calling it "…out-of-control federal spending." Article by Ken Rudin, 25 February 2009. Web resource at https://www.npr.org/sections/politicaljunkie/2009/02/jindal_comment_on_volcano_moni.html

25. Article in *The Atlantic* online titled "Which States Are Givers and Which Are Takers?", showing the GOP's lies about which states are actually on federal 'welfare'. Conservative states far outstrip democratic states as being the worst "Takers" in the nation, with South Carolina taking by far the most of any single state per capita. Article by John Tierney, 8 March 2017. Web resource at https://www.theatlantic.com/business/archive/2014/05/which-states-are-givers-and-which-are-takers/361668/

26. YouTube video of a CNN commentator Alisyn Camerota interviewing Trump voters in late 2017. One of the voters said that he would believe Trump over Jesus. This is the

utter abdication of critical thinking that is endemic among those who support corrupt authoritarian fascists like Trump. Web resource at https://www.youtube.com/watch?v=t28TXvRPpW8

Made in the USA
Monee, IL
07 January 2024

51362492R00049